You Can Draw

PETS

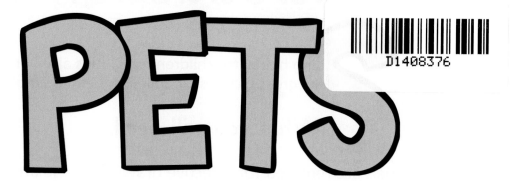

HINKLER
BOOKS

Damien Toll

Introduction

Drawing is a fun and rewarding hobby for children and adults alike. This book is designed to show how easy it is to draw great pictures by building them in simple stages.

What you will need.

Only basic materials are required for effective drawing. These are:

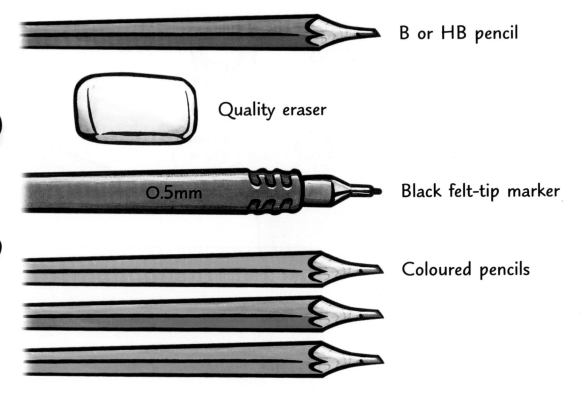

B or HB pencil

Quality eraser

0.5mm   Black felt-tip marker

Coloured pencils

These will be enough to get started. Avoid buying the cheapest pencils. Their leads often break off in the sharpener, even before they can be used. The leads are also generally too hard, making them difficult to see on the page.

Cheap erasers also cause problems by smudging rather than erasing. This often leaves a permanent stain on the paper. By spending a little more on art supplies in these areas, problems such as these can be avoided.

When purchasing a black marker, choose one to suit the size of your drawings. If you draw on a large scale, a thick felt-tip marker may be necessary. If you draw on a medium scale, a medium-point marker will do and if on a small scale, a 0.3mm, 0.5mm, 0.7mm or 0.8mm felt-tip marker will best suit.

The Stages

Simply follow the lines drawn in orange on each stage using your B or HB pencil. The blue lines on each stage show what has already been drawn in the previous stages.

1.

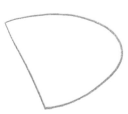

2.

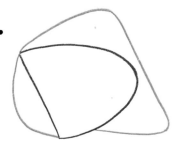

3.

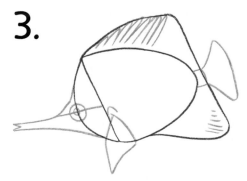

In the final stage the drawing has been outlined in black and the simple shape and wire-frame lines erased. The shapes are only there to help us build the picture. We finish the picture by drawing over the parts we need to make it look like our subject with the black marker, and then erasing all the simple shape lines.

4.

Included here is a sketch of the butterfly fish as it would be originally drawn by an artist.

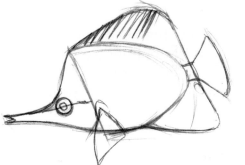

These are how all the animals in this book were originally worked out and drawn. The orange and blue stages you see above are just a simplified version of this process. The drawing here has been made by many quick pencil strokes working over each other to make the line curve smoothly. It does not matter how messy it is as long as the artist knows the general direction of the line to follow with the black marker at the end.

The pencil lines are erased and a clean outline is left. Therefore, do not be afraid to make a little mess with your B or HB pencil, as long as you do not press so hard that you cannot erase it afterwards.

Grids made of squares are set behind each stage in this book. Make sure to draw a grid lightly on your page so it does not press into the paper and show up after being erased. Artist tips have also been added to show you some simple things that can make your drawing look great. Have fun!

The Budgie

The budgerigar is the most popular pet bird in the world. It can be trained to learn words and repeat them in proper sequence. Budgies are an Australian native bird, however the first captive breeding took place in Europe in the 1850s.

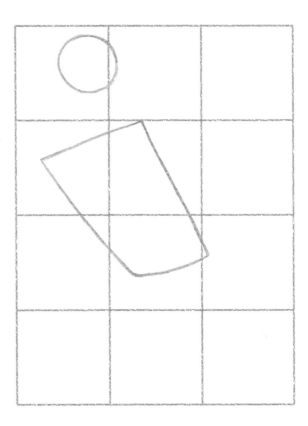

1.

Draw a grid with three equal squares going across and four going down.

Begin with a circle near the top of the grid. Be sure to draw it in the correct position.

Draw a body shape that looks a little like a rectangle that is slightly curved on the bottom and smaller at one end.

2.

Connect the head to the body with straight lines. Notice how the chest of the bird bends just inside the rectangle. This is to eliminate a sharp bend. Draw in the shape for the wing.

Draw the claws. The further set of claws appear above the nearer set. Check your drawing and move on to the next stage.

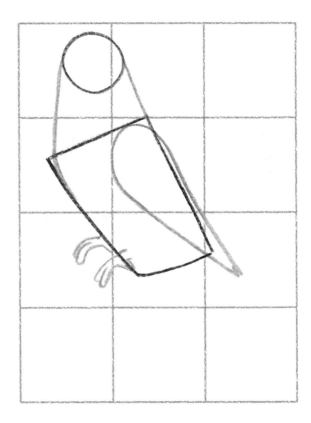

3.

Draw in the beak to the left of the head circle and the eye to the right of the head circle.

Draw in a branch for the budgie to be holding onto. Starting from the back of the rectangle shape for the body, add a long slightly curved shape that comes to a rounded point for the tail feathers.

4.

Outline your artwork, erase the pencil lines and colour to suit. Budgies come in many different colours and patterns. You could add your own colour pattern. Be sure to do it with colour pencil though, as too much black marker will darken the picture, making it look heavy.

The Cat

With around 100 different breeds, domestic cats come in many styles and colours. They are very light-footed and are able to leap seven times their body height upwards. All that exercise makes them tired and they rest about 17 hours a day.

1.

Draw a grid with three equal squares going across and four down.

Begin by drawing the shape for the body. It is basically a backwards "L" with a big long curve joining the ends together.

Draw the head circle above and to the right of the body shape.

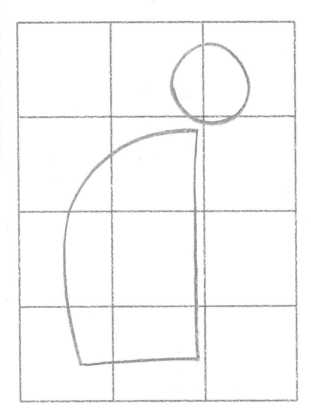

2.

Add some pointy shapes to the head shape for the ears. Draw a small circle inside and near the bottom of the head circle.

Draw an oval leaning on an angle under the head circle. This will become the chest. Join the chest to the bottom right corner of the body shape with a straight line. Check that every thing on your drawing is in the correct position and move on to the next stage.

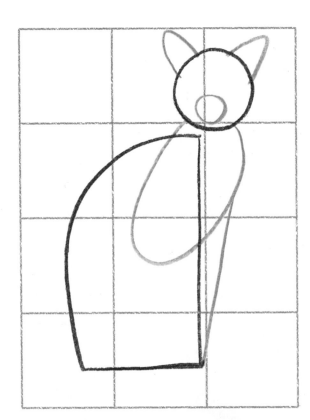

3.

Draw leaf shapes for eyes inside the head circle and add the pupils. Draw a nose in near the top of the small circle inside the head circle. Notice the mouth is a "W" shape.

Draw some lines to show the back leg curving and add in the back foot. Draw a line for the front leg and paw at the bottom. Add the other front paw outside the body shape. Draw in the back of the rear foot and the tail curving around.

4.

Outline your cat and erase the pencil lines. Cats come in many different shapes and colours. You may like to try some different colours and patterns.

Cat-toon

Cats have big eyes and squarish bodies. The domestic cat is the only member of the cat family able to hold its tail high while walking. They can also have a wide head. By emphasising all these points we can turn our cat into a fun cartoon character. The more emphasised the features, the more "cartoony" the character.

1.

Draw a grid with four equal squares going across and three down.

Begin with a shape like an over-inflated football for the head. The top side is more bulgy than the bottom side.

Draw a rectangle at the bottom right side of this for the body.

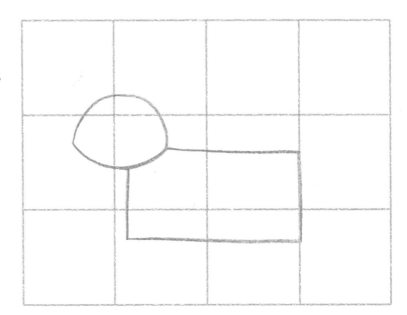

2.

Draw some ears on the head shape. Add a tail on the top corner of the rectangle.

Draw in some legs. Notice that the legs on this side of the cat come right into the rectangle shape.

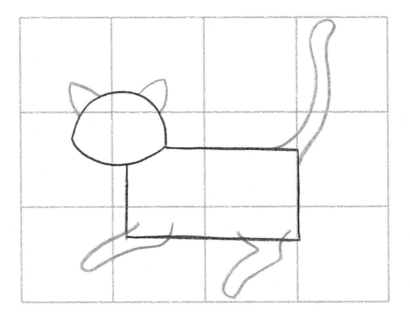

3.

Draw in the face and neck. The bigger the eyes, the cuter the look for the character. Here we have rather large eyes.

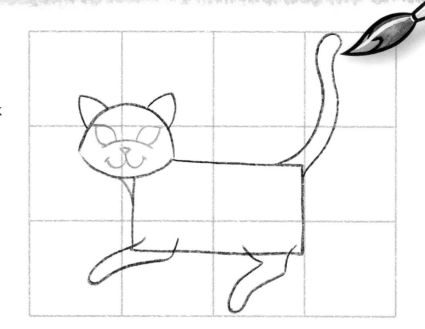

4.

Draw big pupils in the eyes and draw the chin under the mouth.

Draw the legs on the other side of the body.

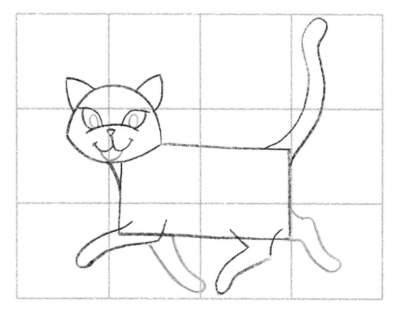

5.

Outline your tabby and erase the pencil lines.

The Horse

The horse has been our helper for thousands of years. Horses were used for everything from plowing fields to general transport. Modern machinery has since replaced most of the duties that horses had to perform. Today the horse is kept for recreation purposes like trail rides and horse shows and sports like polo.

1.

Draw a square grid with three equal squares going across and three down.

Begin with a shape for the body slightly lower than the middle of the grid. Draw a circle for the head at the top left of the grid and join this to the body shape with a line.

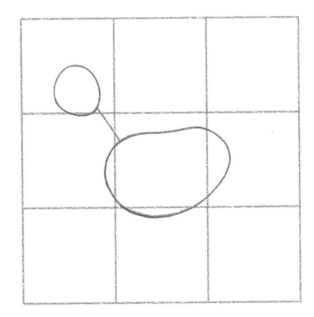

2.

Draw another circle below and slightly to the left of the head circle. Join the circles to make the snout. Draw the part underneath the small circle for the chin.

Draw in the neck, making it fairly thick. Look to see where the neck attaches to the body shape. Draw in some wire-frames for the legs.

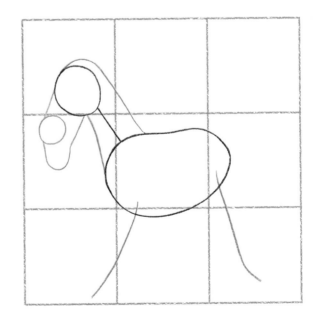

3.

Add the ears and mane to the neck. Draw the horse's eye, mouth and nose.

Draw in the head and body shape for the girl. Draw one leg over the horse's body shape.

Add a wire-frame for the tail of the horse. Draw in the legs and knees around the leg wire-frames.

4.

Draw a wavy line for the white patch on the horse's head.

Add the girl's face, arms, hands and clothes. Draw the reins from her hands to the horse's mouth and around the horse's head.

Draw in the saddle and tail. Draw the legs on the other side of the horse. Notice they do not appear as long as the ones on this side.

5.

Outline the drawing with your marker and erase the pencil lines. This picture is fairly complicated, but with a little practice this drawing technique will become second nature.

Dalmatian

The Dalmatian is a large, friendly, intelligent and energetic dog. They were originally bred for show. They would run ahead of carriages pulled by horses. They also guarded the horses in the stables when they were resting. Dalmatians are easily recognised by their black spots. They are actually born white and do not get their spots until later in life.

1.

Draw a grid with four equal squares going across and three down.

Start with an oval for the body shape. Notice that this oval is on an angle and is smaller at one end.

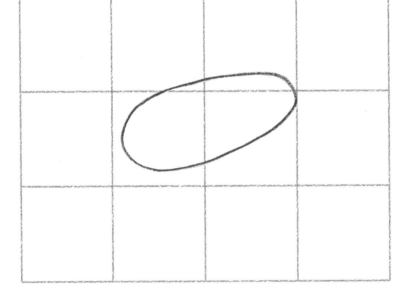

2.

Draw in a circle for the head and join it to the body with a wire-frame.

Add some wire-frames for legs. The back leg is curved.

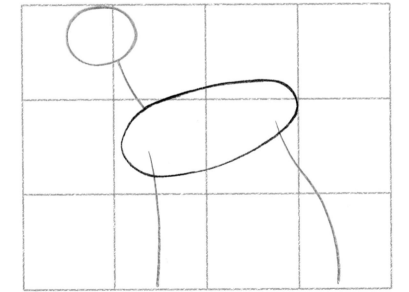

3.

Draw a snout on the head circle and a triangular ear at the back of the head circle.

Draw a sharp tail at the end of the body shape. Draw legs around the wire-frames with lumps for paws at the bottom.

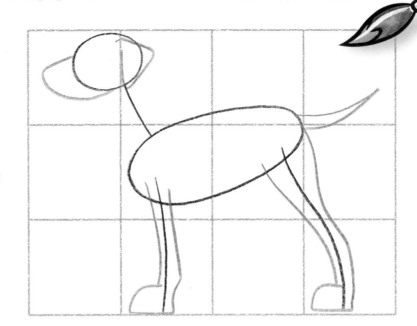

4.

Draw the mouth, eye and eye patch. The eye and eye patch are also triangle shaped. Add spots to the body.

Draw in the legs on the other side of the body, making them a little shorter. Divide up the paws with some curved lines to form toes.

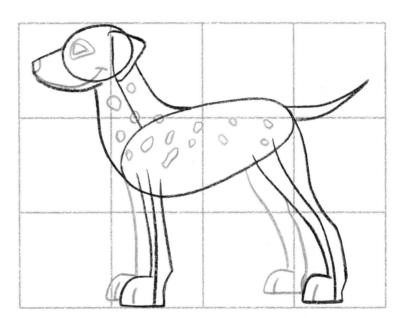

5.

Outline your dalmatian with your marker and erase the pencil lines. Dalmatians are white but can be shaded with a grey or black pencil. Notice the shading under the belly and inside the legs.

Basset Hound

The Basset Hound is a short, large-bodied dog. They were originally bred in England for hunting. With their small legs they could squeeze their way through places larger dogs could not go. Their strong sense of smell meant they could track animals very well. Basset Hounds love companionship and have lots of personality. They are patient and good with children.

1.

Draw a grid with four equal squares going across and two down.

Begin with a shape like a jelly-bean for the body and a circle for the head.

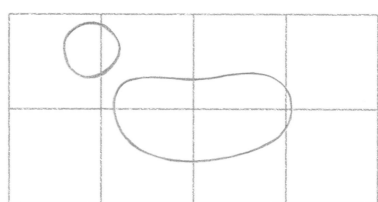

2.

Add a large shape for the dog's snout onto the head shape.

Draw thick legs and big paws. The back leg lines lean towards the right before they travel down to the paws.

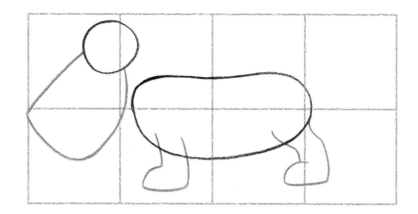

3.

Draw on the neck, joining the head circle and snout to the body.

Draw in the kinked, pointy tail. Add the legs on the other side of the body, making them a little smaller than the ones on this side.

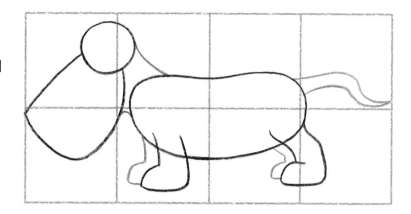

4.

Finally, draw the facial features. A Basset Hound has half-closed eyes with lots of droopy skin underneath them. Add a big smile and some long ears that reach to the ground.

Draw some lines to break up the paws.

5.

Outline your work and erase the pencil lines. When colouring, you may like to try different patches of colour around the body.

Guinea Pig

Guinea Pigs are very small and furry creatures. They are quite timid and often scurry away to hide as they get frightened easily. They have large front teeth. Their teeth never stop growing so they must constantly gnaw on things to wear them down. Guinea Pigs live on vegetables and eat quite a lot. Maybe that is where they got the name "Pigs".

1.

Draw a grid with four equal squares going across and three down.

Draw an oval shape to the right of the grid. This will form most of the bulk of the body.

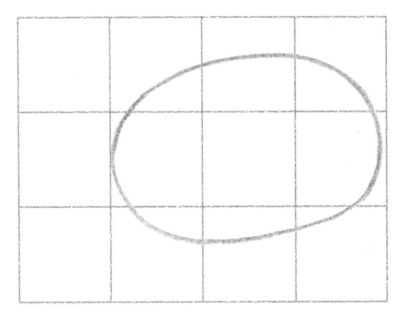

2.

Draw in the more pointy shaped for line the head.

Draw a little lump on the bottom rear of the body shape for the back leg.

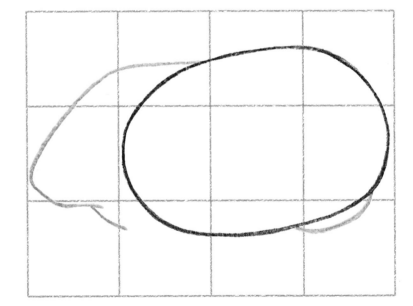

3.

Add the ears, eye and a stretched "V" shape for the nose.

Draw the front legs, making the one further away a little smaller than the one closer to us.

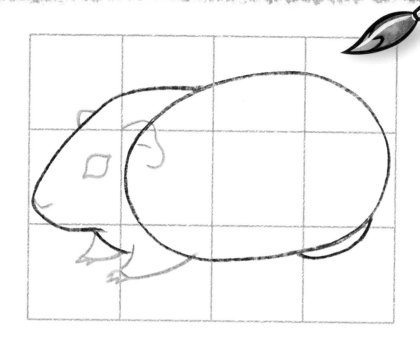

4.

Add the patch around the eye. Draw in a line to show the back of the pupil in the eye. Draw in the front of the ear.

Add some little strokes to show where the coat hair changes colour. Add some little claws to the back foot.

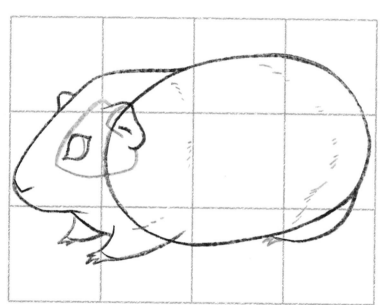

5.

Outline your artwork and erase the pencil lines. Colour your guinea pig.

The Iguana

Iguanas are reptiles. They hatch from an egg and can grow to be the length of an human adult. They are cold-blooded and must spend time in the sun to warm up. They do not respond to owners' commands like other pets. They prefer to be in a quiet and calm environment. Iguanas are able to live with other animals, but they are not playful.

1.

Draw a grid with four equal squares going across and three down.

First, draw in an oval on an angle for the body. This oval is slightly larger at the front.

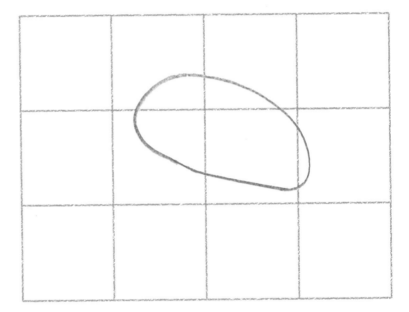

2.

Draw a head shape that is mostly circular, but pointy at the front. Join this to the body shape with a wire-frame.

Draw a long, pointed tail coming off the back of the body shape.

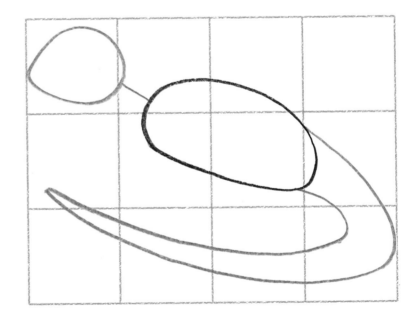

3.

Draw the face within the head shape. Add a triangular flap under the chin. Draw in the back of the neck.

Draw a line from the top of the head to the tail above the neck and body shape. Draw the individual spines on its back to this height. Add the legs and the feet.

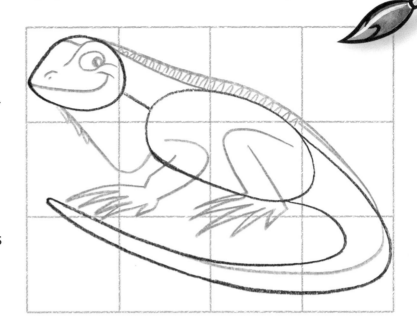

Line shows how high to make the spines

As the line gets closer to the body, the spines gradually get smaller

Artist Tip:

Like our basic shapes, sometimes lines are used just as a guide. The line drawn above the neck that runs down to the tail is only there to show us how high the spines on the back should be. With this line as a height guide, we can simply draw the spines straight up to this height and know that when the line is erased, the drawing will look correct.

4.

Outline your iguana, erase the pencil lines and colour.

The Turtle

Turtles make great pets. They can be kept in a tank that is half water and half dry soil, rocks or sand. Some turtles can breathe under water and some need to come to the surface to take in air. Turtles need some sunlight for their shells to harden. They shed their shell as they grow. Female turtles are generally larger than male turtles but males have longer tails.

1.

Draw a grid with four equal squares going across and three down.

Draw an angled oval shape for the head on the left side of the grid. Check that it is in the correct position before going on to stage two.

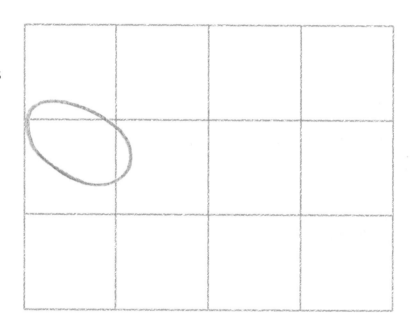

2.

Draw in a big arc for the top of the shell. Draw a dipped double line for the shell edge. Draw a line for the under shell.

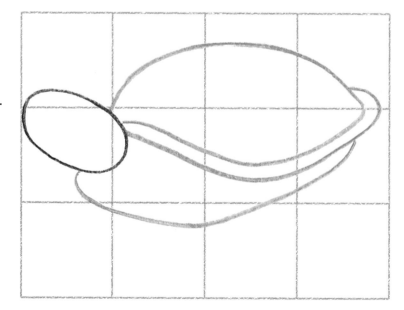

3.

Draw a smile on the lower part of the head circle and an eye above the smile.

Divide the shell into squares stretched across the shell top. Draw in the flippers and lines for the top of the under shell.

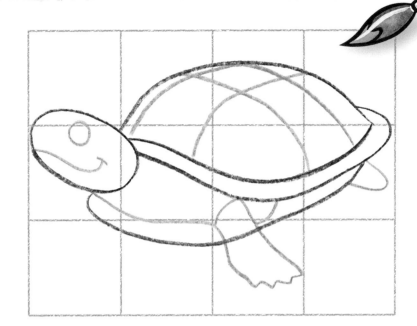

4.

Draw the eye and some lines around it. Add the neck.

Draw in the flipper on the far side. Add a few shapes for the patterns on the flippers, neck and shell top.

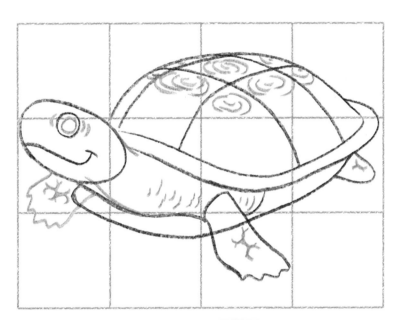

5.

Outline your turtle with your marker and erase the pencil lines. Colour your drawing with greens and yellows.

Butterfly Fish

The Long Nose Butterfly Fish is found in warm tropical waters around coral reefs. It uses its long nose to pick at food pieces between delicate branches of coral where other fish cannot reach. It is a carnivore which means it only eats meat. Its favourite food is small crustaceans. It is a gentle-natured fish that can be kept as a pet in saltwater aquariums.

1.

Draw a grid with four equal squares going across and three down.

Begin with a shape that looks like the letter "D" leaning backwards. This will make up the bulk of the body.

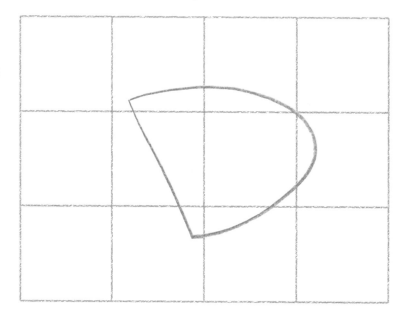

2.

Draw a curve around the front of the "D".

Add another line behind the "D" that has round but sharper corners. Notice where it attaches to the body underneath.

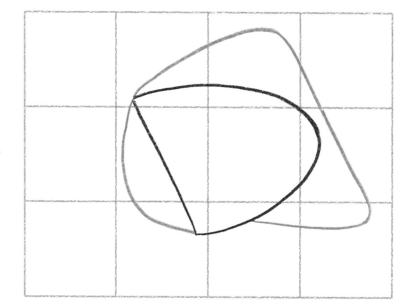

3.

Add a long snout and an eye onto the front of the curve. Divide the head lengthways above the long nose with a straight line.

Add the fin, tail fin and a circle under the tail fin. Divide the top fin into individual spines placed almost to the corner. Draw lines for the bottom fin at the rear.

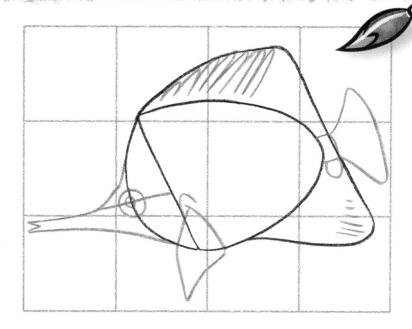

Artist Tip:

Shading can make a drawing look three dimensional. Shading is generally the underside of something where it is not in direct sunlight. When shading, use a darker hue of the same colour. Here a dark yellow has been used for the shading on the lower part of the body which curves under.

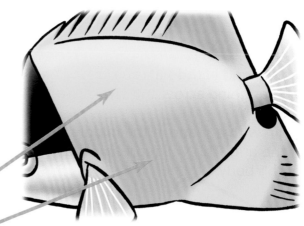

Normal yellow colour

Shaded with a darker yellow
on the underside

4.

Outline your drawing and erase the pencil lines. The colours are very definite on this fish. Use black and white for the head and yellow for the body.

Clown Loach

The Clown Loach is a freshwater fish. They live in a tropical climate where the water is warm. The Clown Loach eats a variety of foods including worms, crustaceans and plants. Because of their colour pattern they are a very popular fish for aquariums. They are a timid fish and like to have members of the same species in tanks with them.

1.

Draw a grid with four equal squares going across and two down.

Begin with a shape in the middle of the grid. This will represent the loach's body.

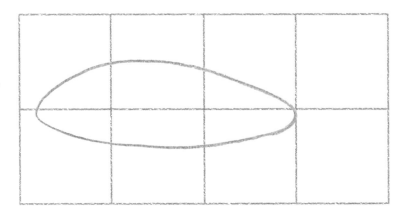

2.

Add a more pointy front to the fish's face for the mouth.

Draw the fins around the body. Notice where the fins are in relation to the body shape. They are further back than you might think.

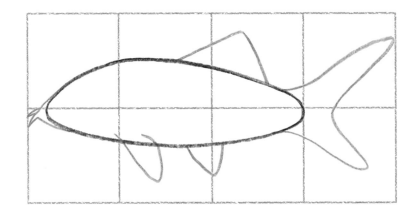

3.

Draw in the mouth and the eye shape. Draw a band around the body. Divide up the top fin with some strokes for spines.

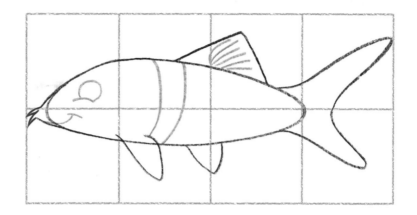

4.

Add the rest of the bands around the body.

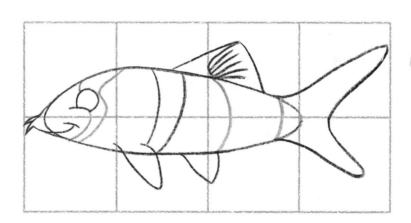

5.

Outline your work and erase the pencil lines. Colour your drawing with black, yellow and orange, adding detail to the fins and tail.

Chimpanzee

Chimps live in trees and are found in family groups. Many of these family groups living together make up a community. Chimps communicate with facial expressions and by clapping their hands. They do not have tails like monkeys but they do have large ears. They eat fruit, leaves, flowers and insects and will sometimes hunt other animals for meat. Some chimps live in santuaries where families can "adopt" them, providing money for their food and care.

1.

Draw a square grid with three equal squares going across and down.

Draw a circle left of the middle of the top of the grid for the head. Draw a big arc going from one side of the grid to the other with a flat bottom. This is the overall shape of the chimp.

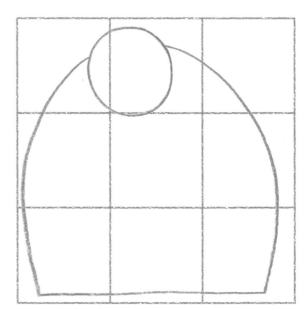

2.

Draw an oval shape below the head circle, making sure to overlap it.

Draw in the "club" shapes for the legs. The legs are bent so we only see the lower legs. Check your drawing for correct placement of shapes on the grid and move on to the next stage.

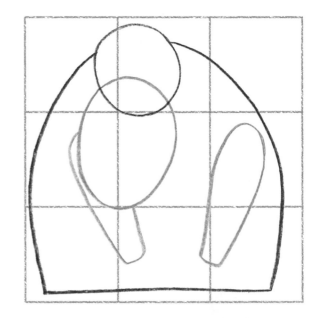

3.

Some details can now be added. Start with the eyebrow, which overlaps the head. The mouth divides the bottom circle in half and the lips stick out of the circle.

Draw in the lines for the arms on either side of the arc. Finish this stage by drawing in shapes for the feet.

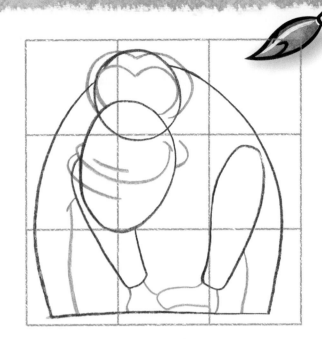

4.

Draw large ears on either side of the head. Put in the eyes and nose. The upper lip is divided with a centre line.

Draw in the top of the arm on the right and the legs near the stomach. Add the hands and lines for the buttocks. Divide the feet up into toes and get your felt-tip marker ready to outline.

5.

Chimps have dark brown or black fur. Here the fur has been coloured in black with a blue/grey highlight on it as a shine. The stomach, hands and face do not have hair on them.

The Python

Pythons are non-venomous snakes that constrict their prey. They wrap themselves around their catch and squeeze until there is no breath left in it. They then unhinge their jaw and eat their prey whole. Pythons are very good swimmers. They spend a lot of their time in the water. Pythons can live for up to 30 years.

1.

Draw a grid with four equal squares going across and three down.

Begin with a wavy line. This line is a wire-frame which the entire body will be based around. It is just like the snake's backbone.

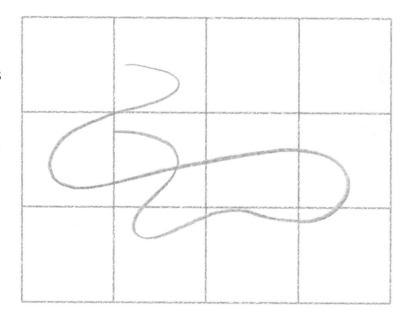

2.

Draw in the snake's body around the wire-frame, making sure to make it fairly thick but parallel to the wire-frame.

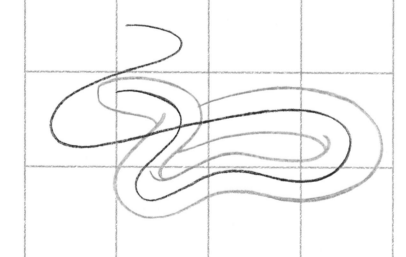

3.

Add the back of the body, gradually getting thinner to a pointy but rounded tail tip.

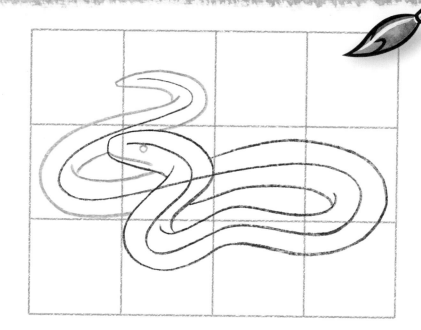

4.

Draw the body pattern around the snake. See if you can make the pattern look like it is on the snake's back.

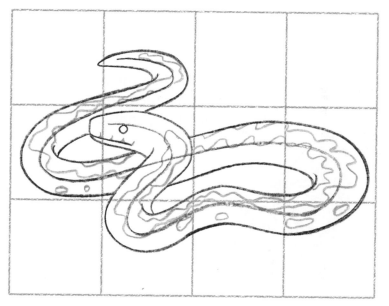

5.

Outline your drawing and erase the pencil lines. The snake is a tan colour with a brown pattern. The pattern has black on its edges.

The Mouse

Mice are a small, friendly pet. They are cheap and easy to care for. They like to be around other mice and have toys to play with. Like Guinea Pigs, their teeth never stop growing so they gnaw on things to wear them down. Mice will eat almost anything. They reproduce very quickly. A female can have 100 babies in a year.

1.

Draw a square grid with three equal squares going across and down.

Begin with a circle for the head in the correct position on the grid. Draw in a rectangle with rounded edges for the body shape.

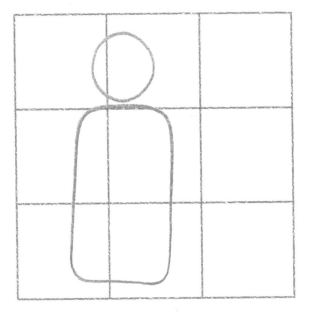

2.

Add another circular shape for the ear on top of the head. Draw an extra shape coming out of the head circle for the snout. Join the head circle to the body shape.

Draw in some shapes for the legs either side of the bottom of the rectangle.

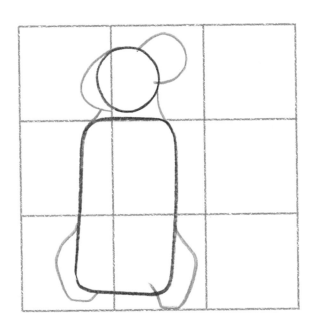

3.

Draw the "V" shaped nose and cheeks that turn into the smiling mouth.

Draw in the eye. Draw in the far ear and inner ear on this side. Add the tiny feet and the line for the tail.

4.

Add the pupil of the eye. Draw the arms and hands holding the cheese. Add the other side of the tail, bringing it to a rounded point.

5.

Once you have outlined the picture and erased the pencil, put in a few selective whiskers coming from the whisker spots. Do not put too many in as it will darken the drawing too much.

Check out these great titles in the *You Can Draw* series!

Published in 2009 by
Hinkler Books Pty Ltd
45–55 Fairchild Street
Heatherton Victoria 3202 Australia
www.hinklerbooks.com

HINKLER
BOOKS

Written and illustrated by Damien Toll

ISBN: 978 1 7418 5329 2

Printed and bound in Malaysia